Positively Chronic

Inspiration for Living Well with Your Chronic Condition

Jilly Hyndman

HEARTRAGEOUS
PUBLISHING

Copyright © 2021 by Jilly Hyndman. All rights reserved.

No part of this publication may be reproduced, distributed or transmitted in any form or by any means, including photocopying, recording, or other electronic or mechanical methods, without the prior written permission of the publisher, except in the case of brief quotations embodied in critical reviews and certain other non-commercial uses permitted by copyright law. For permission requests, write to the author at: hello@jillyhyndman.com

Jilly Hyndman
Heartrageous Publishing
www.jillyhyndman.com

Positively Chronic: Inspiration for Living Well with Your Chronic Condition / Jilly Hyndman —1st ed.
Book: ISBN 978-1-7779005-0-2
E-book: ISBN 978-1-7779005-1-9

I created this little book to help you
live *positively*
with your chronic condition.

Because we all have *those days*:
the ones that are *oh-so*-frustrating,
that get us down, that make us
wonder why we even bother. Ugh!

Sometimes, all we need is a little
encouragement and *inspiration*.

A way to interrupt our
swirly thoughts.

A reminder that we can
do hard things.

And that we've got *support*.

To you, living well, *Jilly*

Contents

How to use this book	vi
Disclaimer	ix

The Prompts

Mindset & Inner Resources	1
Creativity & Meaning	19
Body, Movement & Rest	37
Environment & External Influences	55
Connection to Spirit, Nature & Other Humans	73
Little Luxuries	91

Acknowledgements	109
About the Author	111

How to use this book:

This book contains prompts and practices to help you live well with your chronic condition.

When you feel challenged or just want some inspiration or encouragement, flip to any page.

If the prompt resonates, go ahead and do it. If it doesn't speak to you, flip to another page. Easy peasy.

Adapt and modify the prompts to fit your own needs, abilities and circumstances.

The prompts are grouped into six themes, and listed in no particular order.

Some days, you may feel like doing a page from each theme. Other days, you might be up for just one activity chosen randomly. It's totally up to you!

If you have a printed copy, tuck the book into your bag as you head out for your day. If you've got the electronic copy, keep your device handy and flip through it when you need a midday boost. Share it with a friend who could use a little pick-me-up, too!

Mindset & Inner Resources

...because how and what we think and feel matters and is within our command

...because we all need inspiration, self-expression and for our lives to mean something

Creativity & Meaning

Body, Movement & Rest

...because our bodies are wise, movement moves more than just our bodies and rest is vital

Environment & External Influences

...because our surroundings and what we welcome into our lives impact our well-being

...because it's all connected and we are all divine

Connection to Spirit, Nature & Other Humans

Little Luxuries

...because we all deserve pampering once in awhile and for things to feel a little easier

Disclaimer:

This little book is intended to support and supplement your ongoing professional medical care and treatment. It is not a substitute for or intended to provide, replace or supersede medical or psychological advice or treatment.

Activities suggested here may not be appropriate for all chronic conditions or all people, so please use your own best judgment. If in doubt, please consult with your care team prior to use.

We are all dealing with unique realities at any given time, so adapt and modify these prompts to best fit your current mood, your physical, emotional and mental abilities, and your capacity.

You know yourself best,
so make this work for you!

This book is written from my personal perspective, identity and lived experience as a 40-year Type 1 diabetic, who is managing depression and anxiety, with relative privilege.

Since you will read this book through the lens of your own perspective and lived experiences, I welcome feedback and suggestions for improving the content to better serve those with differently-abled bodies and minds, different access to financial and social supports, and different experiences with the medical system.

x

Mindset & Inner Resources

Mindset & Inner Resources

Take a deep breath.

Then two more.

Ask yourself:
"What do I need in this moment?"

Listen for the wisdom within, then act on it.

Mindset & Inner Resources

When things suck, stop and articulate exactly what sucks.

Acknowledging what is hard, frustrating or disappointing helps diffuse its power.

Mindset & Inner Resources

When you find yourself in a negative thought vortex, pause.

Focus on the experience of one of your senses for 10 seconds. Repeat if needed.

Then choose a thought that serves you better from this calmer, more grounded place.

Mindset & Inner Resources

Practice naming the emotions you experience.

When we are clear about what we are feeling, we can allow those emotions to flow through us instead of getting blocked.

Mindset & Inner Resources

Track your negativity triggers: situations, conditions and people that send you into doom-and-gloom thinking.

Remove, limit or mitigate their presence in your life.

Mindset & Inner Resources

When you hear yourself complaining, flip the complaint into a request.

For example, "I hate that I can't eat butter or I'll have a bad reaction" becomes "Can you leave the butter out of that dish so I don't have a flare up?"

Notice how much more empowered you feel.

Mindset & Inner Resources

Practice connecting to your Inner Leader: the wise, compassionate, clear voice within.

Listen to the wisdom that lives deep within.

Then act accordingly.

Mindset & Inner Resources

When feeling stuck, find an object and consider its traits and characteristics.
For example, a rubber band is flexible and snappy.

Choose one aspect from which to see your situation in a new light.
How could you be flexible or snappy right now, like that rubber band?

Mindset & Inner Resources

Notice when your Inner Critic is getting loud: that internal voice of judgment and fear.

Thank them for their care, then switch channels and turn up the volume of your Inner Leader's wisdom and love.

Mindset & Inner Resources

When a challenge arises, practice observing it like a scientist or documentary filmmaker.
Narrate what you see, including the emotions you're experiencing.

Creating some distance from the emotional experience can help you get unhooked from the drama, and see things more clearly.

Mindset & Inner Resources

Notice where you automatically judge a situation as "good" or "bad."

Become aware of the judgments that fill your day (without judging yourself!).

Just observe and notice what begins to shift from the noticing.

Mindset & Inner Resources

Scan the big challenges you've encountered in life. What did you do to overcome them?
Who did you become in those moments?

Congratulate yourself for getting through those tough times, and see if there's a past lesson to implement in your situation today.

Mindset & Inner Resources

If you're struggling, bring to mind someone you admire: a person in your life, a public figure, or even a character from a movie or book.

Imagine having a conversation with that person and receiving advice, affirmation or encouragement from them.

Mindset & Inner Resources

When something "bad" or unplanned happens,
ask yourself:
What is the gift in this situation?
What can be learned, grown or appreciated about it?

This new perspective can ease your resistance and help you find a way forward.

Mindset & Inner Resources

If you're feeling discomfort, visualize the sensation as a physical object with texture, temperature, colour, weight.

Then imagine surrounding it in golden light, or dipping it in warm honey.

Feel the sensation change as you bring soothing focus to it.

Creativity & Meaning

Creativity & Meaning

Read an autobiography or memoir of someone who lived through a challenging experience.

Draw parallels to your own situation to find inspiration.

Get suggestions from your local library or bookstore.

Creativity & Meaning

Write an email of inspiration, appreciation or pride to yourself.

Set it to auto-send a month or two from now, so you'll forget about it...then be delighted when you receive it.

Creativity & Meaning

Watch or listen to a stand-up comedian - someone who doesn't propagate racism, sexism, classism, ableism, etc. to get a laugh.

Bonus points if it's someone with the same condition as you!

Creativity & Meaning

Ask friends for their favourite inspirational quotes, poems, books or articles.

Create a file to access when you need a boost.

Both the words and thoughts of each friend will bring you comfort.

Creativity & Meaning

Listen to soothing or uplifting music.

Create or follow a playlist that calms, energizes or inspires you.
(Maybe one of each!)

Find one or two go-to tracks that you know will boost your mood, and have them ready when needed.

Creativity & Meaning

Schedule regular time in your calendar for Disease Dates or Condition Check-ins: sacred time to focus on your condition, treatment and relationship with it all.

Assess what's working, what needs adjustment or attention, and remember to celebrate your successes.

Creativity & Meaning

Make a list or create a collage of all the skills and knowledge you have acquired because of your condition.

Answer the question: Who have I become because of this illness?

Pull it out and reflect on it during especially hard days.

Creativity & Meaning

Collect jokes and memes about your condition.

When we can laugh with others who get what it's like to live with our condition, we feel supported in our shared experience.

Creativity & Meaning

If you're feeling low, write what's behind that emotion.

Don't overthink it, just let the pen or keyboard transfer your feelings to the page or document.

Crumple it up or delete it to help release those emotions.

Creativity & Meaning

Create an avatar or character sketch of your condition: it could be in human, animal, monster or alien form. Draw, doodle or describe it. Identify all its traits and behaviours. Give it a name.

When you feel frustrated, direct your upsetting words and thoughts to this creature.

Creativity & Meaning

Share your story. Write it down or record it, then share it with friends and family or post it online. You could offer to be a guest on a podcast that focuses on your condition.

Sharing can help you make sense of your experiences, growth and challenges, while offering insight and inspiration to others.

Creativity & Meaning

Write a poem or song about what you've learned about living with your condition.

It could be happy or funny.

It could express sadness or grief over what's been lost because of your illness.

It could be about hope.

Creativity & Meaning

Dress up in a costume for the day and go about your business, or maybe just run an errand.

Give people something other than your condition to notice about you.

Document the experience.

Creativity & Meaning

Take photos of all the aspects of your condition: medication, food, appointments for check-ups and treatments, mobility considerations, and so on. Create a collage or photo book and add text to explain the story behind the images.

Bring the reality of what it takes to manage your condition into the light.

Creativity & Meaning

Create an altar or vision board dedicated to your health journey.

Choose a special space in your home to place items that visually, energetically and tangibly support your unique concept of health.

Visit it regularly and reflect on your healthy intentions and practices.

Body, Movement & Rest

Body, Movement & Rest

If you are able, lie down on the floor or on a bed or sit in a chair and do nothing but breathe.

Let your thoughts flow and drift.

Only once you feel settled, return to your day.

Body, Movement & Rest

Support healthy sleep
by creating a simple
bedtime ritual:
wash your face;
brush your teeth;
turn off your devices;
identify three gratitudes
from the day and
one wish for tomorrow.

Body, Movement & Rest

Rub your hands together to warm them, then place them over your eyes, on your shoulders or anywhere else that is holding tension.

Repeat until you feel more relaxed.

Body, Movement & Rest

As your body allows, engage in vigorous movement to get your heart rate up and flood your system with feel-good brain chemicals.

Enjoy a hot or cool shower afterward and dress in something super-comfy as an extra reward.

Body, Movement & Rest

Slowly trace one finger
up and down the digits
of your other hand
as you breathe in slowly
on the upstroke,
and out slowly on the
downstroke.

Slow it down even more
for a second round.

Body, Movement & Rest

Whether standing or in a chair, fold forward at your waist and let your head and arms dangle.

If you're standing, bend your knees a little and gently sway as you enjoy a light stretch.

Stay here as long as you like, then unfold slowly.

Body, Movement & Rest

Drink a glass of water right now even if you're not feeling thirsty.
Notice how your mind and body feel afterward.

If you're not a fan of plain water, keep some lime wedges or a bottle of lemon juice in your fridge to add some zing and make it more palatable.

Body, Movement & Rest

Make yourself an easy and nourishing meal that doesn't require much prep:
cut up some cheese and fruit, gather some olives and nuts, tear some naan or bread, dip into a spread or sauce.

Eat with your fingers, slowly.

No dishes to clean up!

Body, Movement & Rest

If it's accessible to you, receive healing touch, such as massage or energetic healing from a skilled practitioner.

Allow someone's special gifts to bring you comfort.

Body, Movement & Rest

Wind down your body and mind before bed by stretching, reading, meditating, praying, journalling or listening to soft music.

Remove distractions so you can have a restful night.

Body, Movement & Rest

Prepare a hot cup of tea
or bowl of soup.

Let the heat of the vessel
seep into your hands.

Feel it travelling up
your arms, your shoulders
and through your body.

Let the warmth soothe you.

Body, Movement & Rest

If your body allows, lie on your back and swing your legs up the wall. (You can do this with a sofa or chair, too.) Stay this way as long as you like.

Try bringing the soles of your feet together by bending your knees to create a diamond shape and rest here awhile.

Body, Movement & Rest

Throughout your day, notice what feels pleasurable: the texture of clothing; the smell of coffee brewing; the sound of birds.

Pay attention to tiny pleasures and joys that are there all along.

Body, Movement & Rest

When you feel a sense of overwhelm approaching, close your eyes and breathe, focusing on lengthening your exhale.
Then breathe in for four counts, hold for four, exhale for four and hold empty for four.

Repeat this "box" pattern until you feel calmer.

Body, Movement & Rest

When you wake up, before you get out of bed or check your phone, set an intention for the day: something you hope will happen or the way you hope to feel.

Visualize this hope or wish for a moment, then get on with your day.

Environment & External Influences

Environment & External Influences

Clean your closet.

Remove anything that is waiting for your body to change.

Donate items to a shelter, career support service or hold a clothing swap with friends.

Environment & External Influences

Pet something furry and soft: a dog, a cat, a llama (if you know one). Even a fluffy blanket or soft pillow.

Keep petting until you feel your stress, worry or frustration flowing out through your fingertips.

Environment & External Influences

Welcome an easy plant into your home.

Notice the impact of having something green and alive indoors.

If it happens to die, thank it for enlivening and nourishing your space, then get another...maybe one that requires even less maintenance.

Environment & External Influences

On a sunny day, step outside and let the sunlight shine on your skin.

Or, move next to a window to let a sunbeam fall over you.

Soak it in, and notice what shifts in your body, mind and heart.

Environment & External Influences

Move through your home
and identify something
that annoys you:
poor lighting in that corner,
a rickety closet door,
that wobbly table.
Make one improvement to
remove that annoyance.

Allow your home to be a
sanctuary, not another
challenge to face.

Environment & External Influences

Pick up a bouquet of fresh flowers, just because.

Or, if it's within your budget, have them delivered regularly.

Enjoy the beauty and fragrance they bring to your home.

Environment & External Influences

Go outside or open a window and listen to the sounds of nature, even if you're in a city. Train your ears first on the sounds that are nearest to you, and then farthest from you.

What do you notice when you really listen?
If you can't hear, what are the vibrations like?

Environment & External Influences

Turn off all your devices and notifications.

Bask in silence for 5 minutes or 15 or an hour.

Notice what shifts.

Environment & External Influences

Put on your softest, coziest, stretchiest, most comfortable clothing, even if it's ugly or tattered.

Wear it all day; longer if you like. No judgment!

Enjoy the opportunity to feel comfortable and comforted by what you wear.

Environment & External Influences

Open a window in the room you're currently in or all the windows in your home. Let some fresh air in, no matter the season or weather.

Air things out for a while, and notice the impact on how you think and feel.

Environment & External Influences

Put on a fun song and tidy up one small area in your space: clear off a countertop, organize items under the bathroom sink, stack a bookshelf, go through your sock drawer.

Notice how you feel after.

Environment & External Influences

Cancel something in your calendar that feels overwhelming this month. If you need a reason, say: "I need to prioritize my health."

While you're at it, block out some additional downtime so you have space for rest and relaxation in the weeks ahead.

Environment & External Influences

In the evening, turn off the lights in your home.

Switch on a salt lamp, light some candles or a fire (if you have one) to create a soft and soothing glow.

Notice what looks different - literally and figuratively - in this light.

Environment & External Influences

Unsubscribe from email lists and unfollow people or organizations that clog up your inbox or social media feed with negativity or stressful content.

Consider limiting your sign-ups, follows and likes to only the most inspiring and life-giving folks.

Environment & External Influences

Rearrange the furniture in a room or redecorate by changing something small, like curtains, pillows or artwork.

Or make a bolder change by painting one wall.

Try living with it for a day or a week. If you don't like it, change it back.

Connection to Spirit, Nature & Other Humans

Connection

List three things you are grateful for in your life: people, circumstances, experiences or lessons you've learned.

Notice how your energy and outlook shifts.

Connection

Write a thank you card or an email to someone who makes your life better.

Tell them one way they have an impact on your well-being.

Send it.

Connection

Find a garden, flowerbed, field, beach or forest and put your hands and feet in the dirt.

Dig. Squeeze. Sift. Bury. Play.

Let the earth's soil ground you.

Connection

Join an in-person or online support group related to your condition.

Even if you don't share anything, you may feel less alone by hearing or reading other folks' stories in a supportive and non-judgmental environment.

Connection

Collect items from nature: leaves, twigs, feathers, stones.

Arrange them on the ground as you contemplate a challenge.

Leave them behind as you continue with your day.

Connection

When asked, "How are you?" be honest instead of answering with the usual "I'm fine."
Acknowledge that you may be struggling, or okay in some ways and not in others at the same time.

Watch how this deepens trust in your relationships, including with yourself.

Connection

Collect smooth stones. Hold them, rub them, squeeze them and let your worry, frustration or anger flow into them.

Toss the stones into water - a river, the ocean, or even your sink - to cleanse them and release the challenging emotions back to nature.

Connection

Consider your spiritual practice: Do you have one? How active is it?
Could you expand this aspect of your life in a way that supports your chronic condition, in particular?

Notice the questions that arise for you, and sit with them or seek out spiritual guidance.

Connection

Find a favourite tree in your yard or neighbourhood: one that makes you feel grounded and protected.

Visit it often, both in person and in your mind.

Linger there until you feel better.

Connection

When you feel the urge to say "I'm sorry" try saying "Thank you" instead.
For example: "I'm sorry for complaining" becomes "Thank you for listening."

This subtle shift in language will awaken gratitude in your life while releasing self-judgment.

Connection

Stroll through your neighbourhood after dark when the world is quieter and more mysterious.

Let the illuminated homes inspire stories about their inhabitants as you wander.

Connection

Seek teachings from spiritual leaders on the topics of health, resilience and compassion, no matter your or their religious affiliations.

Universal themes and truths aren't bound by a particular doctrine.
Be inspired and comforted by what you find.

Connection

When sharing a challenge with a loved one, let them know if you need them to
1. just listen;
2. come up with solutions; or
3. get you into action.

Being clear helps your people support you in ways you most need.

Connection

Find moving water to watch or listen to...a creek, ocean waves or a fountain.

If you don't live near a natural water source, turn on your tap or sprinkler, or get a small desktop fountain.

As you observe, reflect on the life-giving nature and ever-changing shape of water.

Connection

On a clear night,
go outside and look at the
moon and stars.

Notice how the
vastness of the night sky
changes your perspective.

Little Luxuries

Little Luxuries

Treat yourself to a tiny, inexpensive luxury: a single artisan chocolate; a crisp new journal; a lovely handmade soap; or a bouquet of fresh flowers from the grocery store.

Indulge yourself for no reason other than to feel delight.

Little Luxuries

Ask someone to handle a responsibility or decision on your behalf, such as making dinner, mowing the lawn, organizing transportation or childcare or getting groceries.

Allow yourself to be supported by someone who loves you.

Little Luxuries

Wash your face and neck with a warm cloth.

If you have more time, take a generous shower.

If you need a longer escape, run a bath, add some bubbles or oil, dim the lights, play some music and let yourself daydream as you soak.

Little Luxuries

If it's within your budget, hire someone to deep-clean your home, or just a few rooms (like your bathrooms and kitchen).
Or, have your car detailed.

If that's out of reach, wash all your bedding and remake your bed.

Enjoy the results.

Little Luxuries

Gift yourself a yummy scented candle: lavender, rosemary, eucalyptus, vanilla... whatever soothes you.

Light it or simply inhale its fragrance when you need a lift or to relax.

Little Luxuries

Dress up and go on a date with yourself!
Enjoy a meal or drink at a nice restaurant or pack a picnic for the park.
Go window shopping.
Visit a museum or gallery.
Watch live theatre, a movie, or attend a sporting event.
Spend time with yourself doing something special.
Just because.

Little Luxuries

Indulge in a little pampering at a salon, spa or barbershop.

Let someone else take care of you while you relax.

Little Luxuries

Try a new bag, kit or carrying case for your medical gear.

Choose something stylish or fun that brightens your day when you look at it or decorate a plain one with stickers or other embellishments (googly eyes! jewels! glitter!).

Little Luxuries

Make meal time easier: if you can afford it, order in, try a meal-prep service or a ready-to-cook option from a local caterer.

Or, ask a friend to make a dish of theirs you love.

Doing this occasionally can create a little more ease in your life.

Little Luxuries

Create a library of movies or TV shows to watch.

Then spend an afternoon, a full day, or an entire weekend deeply immersed in these stories.

Stay in your jammies and enjoy a few movie snacks, if you like!

Little Luxuries

Buy yourself new underwear and socks and be sure to throw away those ones with holes, fraying bits and missing partners.

Treat yourself to a comfortable and fresh foundation.

Little Luxuries

Get a tattoo of an inspiring quote or image that represents your journey with chronic illness.

It doesn't have to be permanent or expensive! There are tonnes of temporary tattoos with messages and graphics that provide hope or humour.

Little Luxuries

Create a comfort kit: Collect items in a special bag, basket or box that soothe you. Appeal to as many senses as possible: sight (a photo or art object); smell (a lavender satchel); taste (dark chocolate); hearing (a playlist or instrument); and touch (cozy socks or rich lotion).

Little Luxuries

If it's in your budget, enjoy a night or two at a hotel or bed and breakfast (one with room service would be magical!).

A change of scenery or a retreat from everyday life can often give us a renewed outlook on our situation.

Little Luxuries

Sit quietly and imagine the most loving, supportive and kind thing you could do for a friend or loved one.

Is it a gift, an act of service, or some quality time spent with them?

Once you've identified it, do it for yourself!

Acknowledgments

HUGE gratitude and appreciation for all the folks who provided input, encouragement and participated in the Positively Chronic coaching programs so far. Your willingness to share your very personal experiences, struggles and triumphs taught me so much. Thank you for your trust in me and your beautiful perseverance!

To the proofreaders, editors and writing friends who inspire me and made the process fun and final product so much better: your keen eyes and word-ly skills are invaluable.

To my Spiral sisters, who challenge and support me to receive and claim my vision, dare to share it out and offer me unwavering resonant field: my life and work are elevated because of you.

Thanks to my family and friends who have been cheerleaders in so many ways for so many years. Love you all.

And, finally, a thank-you to my chronic conditions. While I would prefer a life free of these diseases, without them, this book wouldn't exist.

About the Author

Jilly Hyndman CPCC PCC, the heartrageous coach, has 40 years experience living with chronic illness. She launched the Positively Chronic Coaching Program in 2020 to provide hope and practical support to others managing chronic conditions. Clients praise her for "being real, especially about the hard stuff" and "relentlessly optimistic." She lives uninvited on the ancestral lands of the Lək̓ʷəŋən people on Vancouver Island with her spouse, child, dog and two snakes and is working on her next book.

Learn more at www.jillyhyndman.com.

www.ingramcontent.com/pod-product-compliance
Lightning Source LLC
Chambersburg PA
CBHW072204100526
44589CB00015B/2356